IMAGES of America
WOODFORD COUNTY

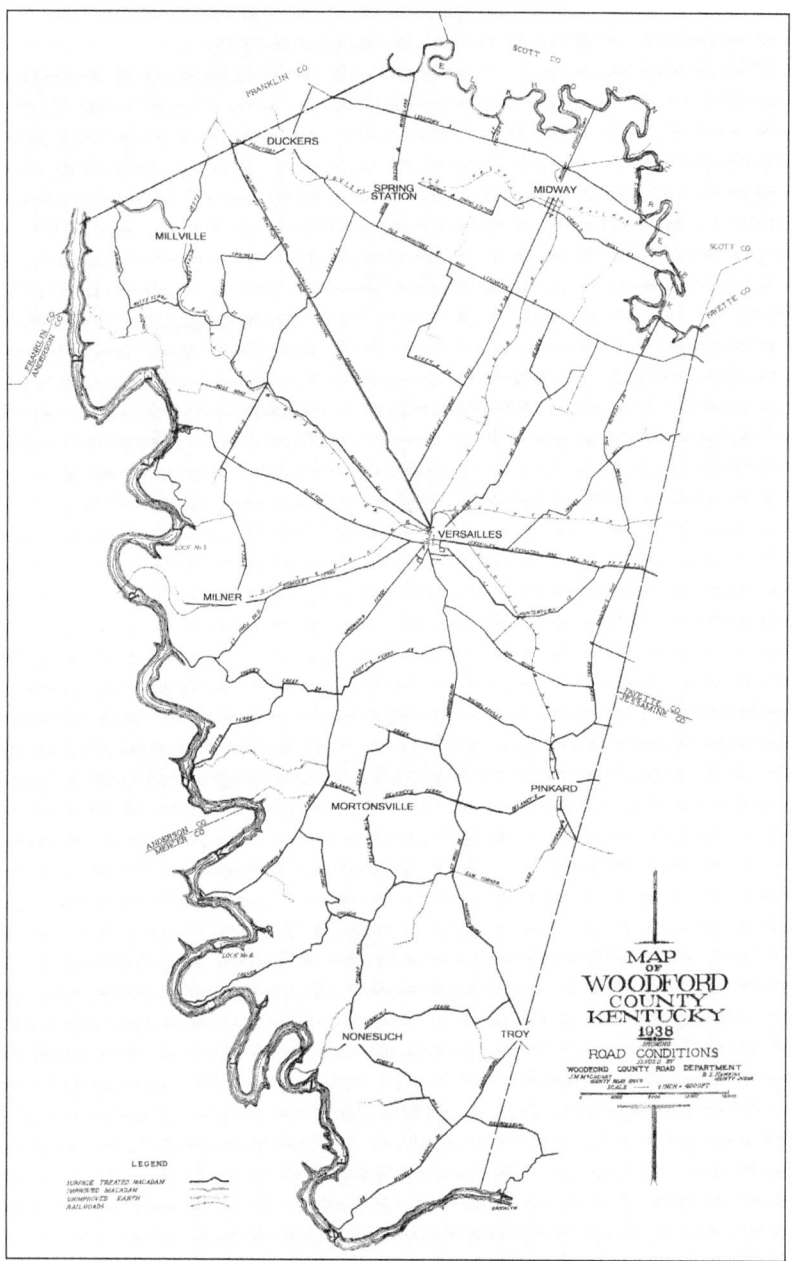

When created in 1788, Woodford was a large county that stretched all the way to the Ohio River. Today, it is a relatively small county located in the heart of the Bluegrass region of central Kentucky. This 1938 county road map shows many of the small communities and roads referenced in this book. (Courtesy of the Woodford County Historical Society.)

ON THE COVER: This c. 1940 photograph shows some men seated at the busiest street corner in downtown Versailles at the intersection of Lexington, Main, and Court Streets. The building in the background is the courthouse. Camp Offutt, shown on the handwritten sign on the light pole, was a Boy Scout camp on the Kentucky River near Shyrock's Ferry. (Courtesy of the Library of Congress.)

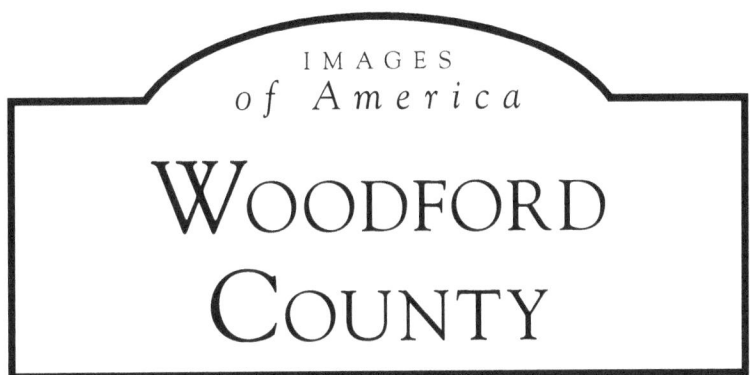

Woodford County Historical Society, Inc.

Copyright © 2020 by Woodford County Historical Society, Inc.
ISBN 978-1-4671-0439-5

Published by Arcadia Publishing
Charleston, South Carolina

Library of Congress Control Number: 2019947038

For all general information, please contact Arcadia Publishing:
Telephone 843-853-2070
Fax 843-853-0044
E-mail sales@arcadiapublishing.com
For customer service and orders:
Toll-Free 1-888-313-2665

Visit us on the Internet at www.arcadiapublishing.com

This book is dedicated to the people of Woodford County, past, present, and future.

Contents

Acknowledgments		6
Introduction		7
1.	Communities	9
2.	Education	23
3.	Interesting People	43
4.	Churches	51
5.	Transportation	61
6.	Business Establishments	75
7.	Farms, Distilleries, and Other Industries	89
8.	Daily Life	105
9.	Distinctive Dwellings	117
Bibliography		127

Acknowledgments

The Woodford County Historical Society's desire to do a publication featuring photographs from its collections became a reality when Arcadia Publishing contacted the society in 2018 about doing a book for its Images of America series. I, then president of the society, became the project chairperson, primarily by default and certainly not by qualifications.

The Woodford County Historical Society thanks the following members for their help: Harold Lee, Linda Finnell, Susan Buffin, Sally Graul, Brenda Jackson, Marti Martin, Eric Petty, and Judy Phillips. These members searched for photographs, conducted research, wrote and proofread text, and performed other tasks.

We would also like to thank other individuals who helped with this book. Mike Timperman was invaluable in scanning and preparing the images. Mike showed up at the society and said he was looking to volunteer for a project. He had only one condition—it had to be interesting. Thankfully he found this project interesting. Thanks to Karoline Manny at Midway University for information on the school and to Phillip Reed for sharing his historical knowledge of southern Woodford County.

Many thanks to our editor at Arcadia Publishing, Caroline Anderson, for her help and valuable feedback, always promptly and cheerfully given. During our introductory conversation, Caroline said, "Relax, it's my job to make you worry less." No one had ever told me that, so I had my doubts. However, she was as good as her word.

Given space limitations, we made the decision that the book would feature photographs from the society's collections. Other than a few select photographs obtained from other organizations, we did not solicit photographs from the community. While the society's photograph collection is broad, it is not exhaustive. Thus, if a particularly notable subject or landmark is not included, it is because it was not in our collections, not that it was unworthy of inclusion.

Unless otherwise noted, all photographs came from the society's collections. Photographs received from other sources are identified, and we thank those sources. We especially appreciate the photographs and information provided by Winfrey Adkins at Nostalgia Station Toy Museum, John Penfield at Bluegrass Railroad Museum, Susan Hughes of the Jouett House, and Bill Penn of the Historic Midway Museum Store.

Information for the text came primarily from the society's files. Works listed in the bibliography were consulted for background information regarding the subjects of the photographs.

—Wayne Basconi
for the Woodford County Historical Society

Introduction

At the time of this writing, Woodford County is 230 years old, making it older than the commonwealth of Kentucky. Originally part of Kentucke County of Virginia, it later became part of Fayette County when the original Kentucke County was subdivided. Finding it difficult to travel to Lexington for court and other government business, residents to the west and south of that city petitioned the Virginia legislature for their own county. In November 1788, the legislature approved the formation of a new county to be formed from within the boundaries of Fayette County that would be called Woodford after Revolutionary War general William Woodford. The new county was quite large, with its boundaries being generally the Ohio River to the north and northwest, the northern portion of the Licking River to the northeast, and the Kentucky River on the west and south. Woodford County was in turn reduced in size by the formation of no less than nine additional counties in whole or in part from within its borders. Thus, by 1800, Woodford County was reduced to the shape and size that it is today; one of Kentucky's smaller counties, it consists of 192 square miles.

Woodford County is located entirely within the geological area known as the Inner Bluegrass, characterized by an underlying dome of Ordovician limestone. The landscape has been described as undulating, being neither hilly nor flat. The limestone near the surface dissolved easily with rainfall, providing a source of calcium for grazing livestock. The surface was not forested at the time of the first white settlers, but was what is referred to as woodland pastures. These were generally open with areas of large trees and cane. This combination made for pastureland that was as good as any found anywhere in the world. It was a landscape ideal for the first settlers to graze their horses and cattle and to establish farms.

It was in this natural setting that Woodford County was established and began to thrive. Its farms soon were producing tobacco, hemp, grains, and quality livestock, primarily cattle and sheep. Later, its stock farms became known for the quality of their horses and mules. By the mid-1800s, some of the finest stallions that formed the foundation of the modern Thoroughbred industry were residing on Woodford County farms.

Industry and business kept pace with the county's agriculture success. Like most communities at the time, the county was pretty much self-contained due to the lack of easy and efficient transportation. Every area of the county was served by gristmills, sawmills, tanneries, distilleries, and rope walks that turned hemp fibers into rope and fabric.

Woodford County did not just engage in these activities but excelled in them in many cases. It was one of the leading hemp-producing counties in the state. It was where the scientific approach to making bourbon was perfected at the hands of James Crow, a Scottish physician and chemist who made his way to Woodford County and went into the distilling business. A hundred years before the establishment of the modern Kentucky Bourbon Trail, folks from eastern cities were taking trains to come visit an elegant distillery near Millville in Woodford County.

This business activity has continued until the present time. Woodford County is still a major agricultural center with cattle and horse farms, many with international reputations for the quality of their stock. It has two operating distilleries, wineries, and even an operating flour mill. It also has much modern industry with manufacturing and distribution centers. As a consequence, it remains one of the state's more prosperous counties and usually ranks in the top five for the lowest unemployment rate.

Along with this economic activity came those things that make a community. Small communities soon dotted the county, with churches, stores, banks, and shops, followed later by schools, clubs, and other social organizations.

Located between the state capital in Frankfort and the early-settled city of Lexington, Woodford County was in a position to affect both state and national political matters. Its native son John J. Crittenden was a governor of Kentucky, US attorney general, and US senator who tried to prevent the Civil War by working to find a compromise. The county has supplied six governors to the state of Kentucky, more than any other county.

This book of photographs seeks to document this background and history from the mid-1800s through 1950. It might be considered a snapshot of a century in the life of a county, showing people as they go about their daily lives of working, learning, worshiping, and everyday living. There are photographs of some well-known and even famous individuals who made a difference at the national, state, or local level. However, most of the photographs are just of ordinary folks doing what they did in the regular routines of their lives.

One

COMMUNITIES

Today, the only incorporated communities in Woodford County are the towns of Versailles, the county seat, and Midway. They are also the only two post offices left in the county. The community that would become Versailles was selected at the time of the formation of Woodford County in 1789 to serve as the county seat. The town has always served that role. It has always been the hub of the county's government and commercial activity due to the presence of the courthouse and its central location.

Midway was founded in the 1830s, when the company constructing the Lexington & Ohio Railroad decided to establish a town on land it had purchased from John Francisco for the railroad right-of-way. The name came from the fact that it was located halfway between Frankfort and Lexington. Its early streets were named for the owners of the railroad company. It was soon a thriving town with stores and manufacturing concerns, including a jeans factory, ropewalks, and a paper mill. There were also many fine homes built in the town.

Versailles and Midway continue to thrive today and are commercial centers. Yet it would be wrong to consider these as the only communities in the county. A quick look at the map on page two will reveal several villages, some with interesting names such as Duckers, Nonesuch, and Pinckard. While today they are mainly quiet, residential areas, they were nonetheless communities where people lived, worked, and were proud to call home. Many of them at one time or another had a school, at least one church, stores, blacksmith shops, and other businesses. Most of them had a post office at some point, since there were 34 different post offices in the county at different times over the decades. Both Troy and Mortonsville had banks. Troy had an Odd Fellows hall. Communities located on the various railroads, such as Duckers, Spring Station, and Pinckard, had depots where local residents could catch trains to other communities and ship and receive goods.

The photographs in this chapter show the diversity of the communities that have made up Woodford County over the decades.

Woodford County was established on November 12, 1788, by an act of the Virginia legislature. There was of course no courthouse in which to go about setting up the county government and carrying out its governmental activities. The town of Versailles, which would become the county seat, had not even been established yet. Attorney Caleb Wallace offered his law office, shown here, near the present town of Midway, for county officials to use. On May 5 and 6, 1789, the first sessions of the county court of Woodford County met in this modest building. The court adopted procedural rules, appointed county officials, and adopted ordinances to run the county. Subsequent sessions were held at the Woodford Presbyterian Church, of which Wallace was the pastor. Wallace (1742–1814) was a talented individual with many different interests. He was a pastor, a lawyer, and a justice on the Kentucky Court of Appeals. He was also involved in establishing various colleges, including what would become Transylvania University. The building shown here was torn down around 1917.

Directly behind the courthouse in Versailles, water gushed out of the side of the hill in such volume that the valley below it was known as Big Spring Bottom. It was the site of a distillery and was also the first source of Versailles's water supply. The spring still flows today, although with nothing like the volume shown in this 1940 photograph.

There have been four different courthouses at the same location in Versailles. The first was a log cabin that was replaced in 1794 by a small stone building. The third courthouse, shown here, was completed in 1813 and underwent many additions. This photograph was taken around 1900 looking south down Main Street. The courthouse had been enlarged and modified in the early 1880s.

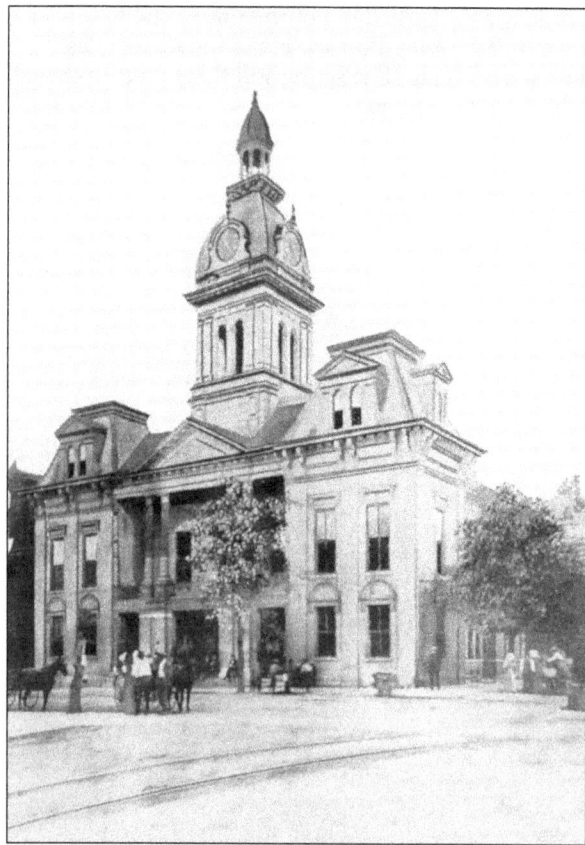

This is a 1926 view of the third courthouse and shows the front of the building. The view is from the northeast corner of Lexington and Main Streets. The interurban's electric railroad tracks can be seen in the foreground. Other than a few exterior details, the building had not changed much in the 25 years since the preceding photograph was taken.

It is estimated that there were a total of seven modifications or expansions to the 1813 building that was the third courthouse. This photograph, with the board construction fence around the building, was taken while the courthouse was undergoing renovations in 1941. This was the last of the renovations to the building.

This 1949 photograph shows the final configuration of the third courthouse after the various additions and changes to the building and clock tower. The building would burn 16 years later in 1965. Of interest is the Versailles Police Department cruiser sitting to the right of the courthouse. The brick county jail can be seen behind the courthouse.

Main Street in Versailles is pictured in 1914 looking to the south. The courthouse is on the right, with the Amsden Bank building in the background on the same side of the street. Lexington Street can be seen at left. Both horse-drawn carriages and early automobiles can be seen in the street. The tracks of the interurban electric trolley that connected Versailles with Lexington and Frankfort (see page 63) can just be made out at lower left.

This 1929 photograph gives a good view of the Courthouse Square looking north from South Main Street. The three-story brick building beside the courthouse is the Odd Fellows hall, which shared the block with the courthouse until 1965, when the courthouse burned. The top floor of the building contained an auditorium where plays and other shows were presented.

This 1940s photograph of Versailles's Main Street shows the changes made during the approximately 30 years since the photograph on the previous page was taken. There are no longer any carriages in the street, and the interurban tracks are long gone. There is a traffic light in front of the courthouse at the intersection of Lexington and Main Streets.

The new Woodford County Hospital is pictured shortly after its opening on March 1, 1909. It was constructed at a cost of $14,000 on Brown Avenue (now Amsden Avenue) on land donated by Lucy Alexander in memory of her late husband, A.J. This building replaced the first hospital in the county, which opened in 1904 on Macey Avenue.

This attractive building at the northeast corner of Main and Morgan Streets is today the Versailles City Hall. Built in 1910 by the federal government, it served as the Versailles Post Office until 1966. That year, the post office was moved to Lexington Street. The exterior of the building today is unchanged from this photograph other than that some windows no longer have awnings.

This 1930s photograph was taken looking west on Montgomery Avenue in Versailles. Montgomery Avenue was created around 1870 when D. Montgomery Megee opened the street through land he owned. It was originally called Megee Street. The photograph shows that the street has not changed much over the years. Today, it remains a pleasant residential street with attractive homes and many shade trees.

This 1920 photograph shows the construction of the first waterline from the Kentucky River to the town of Versailles. The location is on High Street looking toward downtown with the courthouse in the background. The workers appear to be digging through solid rock. Limestone rock is near the surface in central Kentucky, which is great for making bourbon and pasturing Thoroughbred horses, but not for installing underground pipelines.

This photograph of the Logan Helm–Woodford County Public Library on Main Street in Versailles was taken in 1911. The impressive building was completed in 1906, having been designed by the Lexington architectural firm of Copland & Dale. Money for the completion of the building was given by Margaret C. Logan in memory of her nephew Logan Helm. When the library opened in 1906, it had a collection of 1,550 books. Local citizens began to use the library immediately. The library reported that it had 619 registered patrons in its first year. It survived a major fire in June 1907, although only 500 books were saved. The library still uses this building, although it has expanded into an adjoining one.

This c. 1900 photograph shows the Collins Opera House, erected on Railroad Street in Midway by T.C. Collins in 1882. The opera house was on the second floor, which extended over four stores on the first floor. It served as a venue for plays, dances, and many other social events. In 1915, most of the buildings shown burned in a fire. (Courtesy of Bill Penn/Historic Midway Museum Store.)

This photograph shows what today is referred to as the Porter House at 113 North Winter Street in Midway. It was built in 1852 by Dr. Thomas J. Isles, Midway's first doctor, for his daughter. It was later owned by Nathaniel and Susan Porter, who operated a tavern and inn they named the Porter House. This winter view dates to the early 1900s.

Spring Station in northern Woodford County had a post office from 1856 until 1973. The post office building shown here around 1950 originally served as a depot on the Louisville & Nashville (L&N) Railroad, hence the very close proximity to the railroad tracks. This building also served as the corporate office of the Southern Pacific Railroad until it erected its own building in 1939 (see page 73).

There was a post office in Mortonsville from 1828 until 1921. It was on the north side of the main street through Mortonsville (today's Delaney Ferry Road) near the intersection with Carpenter Pike. From left to right in this c. 1910 photograph are John Barnes, Ed Boston, Charlie Orr, unidentified, Lee Dale and his son, and Jim Turner. Lee Dale was the owner of the store shown, where the post office was located.

In 1877, Mortonsville had a population of 744 and several businesses. Today, it is a quiet residential village without any businesses. However, in the 1940s, when this photograph was taken, it had two gas stations across the street from each other. This is a view looking west on what was the main street of the community.

This two-story brick building was the Odd Fellows hall in the community of Troy in southern Woodford County. The building is shown on the 1877 D.G. Beers & Co. map of Woodford County and was on the eastern side of today's Route 33 just north of the intersection with Keene Road. The first floor was used as a retail store space. The building burned down sometime after 1901. Although Troy was primarily a farming community, it also boasted stores, a post office, a doctor's office, and a blacksmith shop. The Odd Fellows are a nonpolitical, nonsectarian fraternal organization founded in the early 1800s.

Two

EDUCATION

No history of Woodford County would be complete without including the development of schools and other educational institutions. The earliest schools were private, usually associated with churches. Only those children whose parents had the resources and inclination to send them to school received a formal education. Kentucky being a slave state, the children of slaves generally did not receive any formal education, although some slave owners may have provided some limited education to selected individuals.

Gradually that began to change, with public education becoming the norm rather than the exception. After slavery was ended by the 13th Amendment in 1865, African American children eventually started to receive some formal education, albeit in segregated schools. As early as 1867, freedman schools were established in Versailles and Midway for educating African American children.

The first public school was organized in Versailles in 1875. Rural areas were generally served by one- and two-room schoolhouses. Eventually, any student wanting to attend public school could do so. However, private schools continued to exist, often to serve special needs. The Cleveland Home for Orphans, the Kentucky Female Orphan School at Midway (today's Midway University), the Massie School, and Margaret College/High School are some examples.

This chapter looks at the early years of public and private education in Woodford County and how education has changed over the years.

Melvin Hifner was born in 1856 in the small Woodford County village of Troy. He studied civil engineering in college but instead became a teacher. In 1881, at the age of 25, he was appointed Woodford County school superintendent, a job he would hold for the next 45 years. During part of this time, he also served as county road superintendent, thus making use of his engineering training. One of the most interesting things that Hifner did as school superintendent was having all of the schools in the county, both public and private, photographed in 1892. There was a total of 42 schools. The photographs were to be exhibited at the World's Columbian Exposition of 1893 in Chicago. They provide excellent documentation of the state of Woodford County schools in the late 1800s. Space limitations do not allow all of the 1892 photographs to be included, but a representative sample of 12 is shown on the following pages.

In 1892, because Woodford County schools were segregated, there were 11 African American schools. Shown here is the Jacksontown School with students and teachers. Jacksontown was on the western edge of Versailles. The exact location of this long-gone building could not be determined, but it is believed to have stood on the north side of Tyrone Pike (Route 62) and just east of the current Simmons Elementary School.

This was the Mount Edwin School, on Oregon Road near the intersection with Patterson Road. Superintendent Hifner not only arranged for the schools to be photographed, he also appeared in several of the pictures. He is seen here on the far left near the trees.

The school in Midway was started in 1869 by Eugenia Williams and was supported by the Town of Midway. The school changed locations a few times before moving here to the western end of Bruen Street in 1887. Once again, Superintendent Hifner is in the photograph, standing off by himself on the right. Today, the building is the home of the Midway Methodist Church.

This was the Pisgah School, which was on the north side of today's Route 60 a quarter-mile east of the Huntertown Road intersection and just to the west of Pisgah Pike. Superintendent Hifner is at center, standing behind the fence. The taller boy at the left front is holding a dog, who does not seem to be enjoying having his photograph taken.

This trim-looking building was the Clear Creek School. It was near the intersection of Pinckard Pike (Route 169) and Troy Pike (Route 33). It probably faced Pinckard Pike. The headwaters of Clear Creek are located nearby, which likely was the basis for the name of the school.

The Grier's Creek School was at the current intersection of Shyrock's Ferry Road and Route 62. The road seen curving in the distance is the Tyrone Pike (Route 62). The building was constructed in 1880 and replaced in 1912. The teacher shown on the left is Mona Jackson.

This African American school was called the Paynes Mill School and was just east of Paynes Depot Road (which in those days was called the Mount Vernon & Paynes Depot Pike). It was near the Fayette County line. This was one of the few two-story school buildings in the 1892 photographs. Two stories were probably required to accommodate the relatively large number of students.

This private school was referred to as the Mrs. Crenshaw Rose Hill Seminary and was at 251 Rose Hill Avenue. It was operated in the late 1800s by Gillie Crenshaw. It later became known as the Rose Hill Female Academy. The building shown was moved to High Street, where it became a residence. The school's commencement exercises were held in the Odd Fellows hall in downtown Versailles.

The Mount Vernon School was at the southwestern corner of Old Frankfort and Pisgah Pikes. The school was across Old Frankfort Pike from the Mount Vernon Baptist Church, whose congregation was first established at this location in 1822. The current church building dates to 1905. The tombstones shown in the photograph are those of the church cemetery. Today, there is a modern residence at the former school site.

This was the Elm Bend School, another small school out in the county. It was on Troy Pike, or Route 33, just south of Elm Corner. As shown by this group, there was a wide range of ages among the students being taught in these schools, which was surely a challenge to the teacher. This building is one of the few from 1892 that is still in existence, although it has long been abandoned.

This was the school at Pinckard, a community at the intersection of Route 169 and Delaney Ferry Road near the Jessamine County line. All of the children in the photograph are holding small American flags. The school would have been on the east side of Route 169, at the site where today there is a former brick schoolhouse that has been converted to a private residence.

The African American school in Mortonsville was located next to the Baptist church, which also served the African American community. Both were on what today is Carpenter Pike where Polk Memorial Baptist Church is located. It is believed that the school is the building to the extreme right of the photograph, of which only the front can be seen. The children are lined up on the side of the church. The Baptist church in Mortonsville was established in 1853. There have been four different buildings at the site; the one in the photograph is the third and would have been built in 1876. The current church at the site, Polk Memorial, was built in 1921.

The Kentucky Female Orphan School was founded in Midway in 1847 with the then-revolutionary idea that female orphans would be given a formal education. L.L. Pinkerton was a young physician and minister in the Christian Church who saw the need for such a school and worked with other citizens to make it a reality. The photograph above is of Pinkerton Hall, built in 1859. Below is Parrish Hall around 1920. In order to relieve crowding in Pinkerton Hall, Parrish Hall was started in 1893 and completed in 1895 at a cost of $25,000. The building contained administrative offices, reception rooms, and some dormitory and dining space. The school later became Midway College and today is Midway University, a four-year co-ed institution. Pinkerton Hall is still in use by the university. Parrish Hall was removed in 1983 due to deterioration.

This photograph of the Clover Bottom School in southern Woodford County was taken on May 3, 1929. Mayme Prather, the teacher, is shown with her students. The school was first occupied in February 1917 and closed around 1935 because of consolidation. The object in the background to the left of the group is a water pump.

This photograph from around 1904 shows students and teachers of Midway High School. The woman in the long skirt on the left is Mattie Hugh. The boy to her immediate left is Pascal Lacefield. Willie Wise is seated on the bench holding a baseball. Esther Epstein is the girl standing behind him. Catherine Wallace Parrish is in the back row on the right. The rest are unidentified.

This c. 1913 photograph shows the student body of the Clifton School. It was located at what was known as Brookie's Crossroads, which is on today's Highway 1964, or Clifton Road. The school closed in 1929 because of consolidation with the Versailles Elementary School. The building was one of the schools photographed in 1892, but by this time, it had been covered with clapboards.

This c. 1910–1911 photograph shows the students at a school in the Brushy Run area in southern Woodford County. Today the area is known as Clover Bottom. Given the distance some students had to travel to rural schools, it was not uncommon for them to ride horses or ponies. The boy on the right decided to include his horse in the group photograph.

This photograph was taken sometime between 1910 and 1920 and shows the Nonesuch School in the southern part of the county. A large number of adults are shown, so apparently it is a photograph of some event taking place at the school. The school would have been on the west side of Fords Mill Road just north of the intersection with Cummins Ferry Road.

The first public school in Versailles was established in 1875 when the city took over a private school on the corner of South Main Street and Macey Avenue. This building was constructed in 1888 on portions of the original building at the site. It served all grades until 1921, when the high school grades were moved to the Childer House on Maple Street. The building was removed in the late 1960s.

Versailles High School opened in 1927 for grades seven through 12. It was located on the corner of Maple and Lexington Streets. It became Woodford County High School in the 1963–1964 school year after merging with Midway High School. The building became a junior high school in 1964, and after a renovation in 1982, became the Woodford County Middle School. The building closed after the 2003–2004 school year and was demolished in 2017.

Margaret Hall was a private school in Versailles that was affiliated with the Episcopal denomination and operated from 1898 to 1979. It primarily served females in grades one through 12, although programs for male students in the lower grades and a junior college for females were offered at various times. The building is listed in the National Register of Historic Places and has been converted to residential use, comprising 51 apartments.

This photograph shows May Day festivities at Margaret Hall School sometime between 1942 and 1944. The May Day queen and her court represented various grades. Among the Versailles students shown are Jean Baker Hamilton (class of 1945), fifth from left; Mary "Woo" McCauley Rasnick (1945), fifth from right; and Betsy Maury Pratt Kelly (1949), seated on the ground.

The Massie School was founded in Lexington by Robert K. Massie in 1919. In 1922, the school moved to Woodford County on what was known as the Cleveland Place, which was also the birthplace of Kentucky statesman John Crittenden. It was two and a half miles east of Versailles on today's Route 60 on the property later occupied by the Methodist Home and now the home of Frontier Nursing University. The Massie School offered a six-year program for boys only. Its primary purpose was to prepare its students for college. Its coursework included English, languages, mathematics, history, physics, chemistry, and other classes. In 1929, it became the Woodford School, which closed in 1931 when the Methodist Home acquired the property. The photograph shows the main building of the school around 1925.

Shown here is the Versailles High School senior class of 1931–1932. These students would have been one of the earliest graduating classes to have completed all of their high school years at the new school, which opened in 1927.

In 1921, a week-long teachers' institute was held at Simmons High School, the African American high school in Versailles. The participants were photographed on the steps of the school. The two children on the left are the sons of Prof. T.J. Smith, who served as principal. The man seated at right is Woodford County school superintendent Melvin Hifner.

Shown here is the Versailles High School football team of 1928. They played their home games behind the high school on what would become known as Memorial Field. This was the second football team at the new high school on Maple Street, which opened in 1927. The team had an undefeated season, going 8-0.

This is the 1931–1932 Versailles High School basketball team. The picture was taken at a side entrance to the school. It was a tough season for these Yellow Jackets. Records available for part of the season show a record of 2-7. They lost to Henry Clay High School of Lexington in the district tournament by a score of 34-14.

Although most photographs of athletic teams from this period show boys' teams, the historical society has this photograph of the 1922 Versailles High School girls' basketball team in their varsity letter sweaters. The word "Champs" on the basketball refers to the fact that they were district champions. Unfortunately, they were eliminated in the first round of the state tournament by Paducah.

The Midway High School Blue Jays won the 1937 Kentucky state basketball championship. Members of the team are, from left to right (first row) Ernest Jefferson, Armon Portwood, Carl Thomas, James Murphy, Jack Penn, and Raymond Sanderson; (second row) superintendent O.B. Dabney and coach G.L. Burns; (third row) manager Tommy Duffy, Quentin Columbia, Karl Jefferson, Sherman Columbia, and Harold Sanderson. Midway was undefeated in the regular season.

May Day celebrations were held at some county schools to celebrate the coming of summer. Included in some of the celebrations was a folk dance around a decorated maypole; the tradition began in Europe. This grade school maypole dance took place on the football field at Versailles High School around the 1930s. The teachers probably looked forward to summer as much as the students.

Three

INTERESTING PEOPLE

Woodford County has its share of famous, almost famous, and ordinary but interesting folks. The Woodford County Historical Society has photographs and portraits of some of these individuals who made a difference in the county, the state, and even in the country. Included are soldiers, statesmen, a leading woman suffragist, businessmen, and individuals of other professions.

Some local people of note lived before the age of photography and did not have their portrait painted; thus the historical society has no image of them. A prime example is Jack Jouett. He was born in 1754 and was a true military hero of the American Revolution. As a Virginia militiaman, he rode 40 miles during the night from Louisa County to Charlottesville to warn Thomas Jefferson, then Virginia governor, and the state legislature that British troops were marching to capture them. The fact that most of the ride was not on roads but was cross-country and in the dark made it a truly daring and difficult undertaking. After the war, Jouett was given a land grant in Kentucky for his military service. He built a house on Craigs Creek in southern Woodford County and lived there for several years with his family. He also represented Woodford County in the Kentucky House of Representatives. Unfortunately, an image of Jouett is not available, but his house still exists in the county (see chapter nine).

Thankfully, there are images of several important and interesting people, as will be seen in this chapter. All of the people presented here have one thing in common: Woodford County. They were born here, lived here, or represented the county in some capacity.

Woodford County was named for Revolutionary War general William Woodford, shown in this portrait. Woodford was born in Caroline County, Virginia, and followed in the footsteps of his military father by joining the Virginia militia. With the coming of the Revolutionary War, Woodford was appointed colonel of the 2nd Virginia Regiment. The regiment became part of George Washington's Continental Army, where Woodford rose to the rank of brigadier general. He led troops in battle in New Jersey before being sent to South Carolina, where he was captured by the British at the siege of Charleston. He was held on a British prisoner ship in New York, where he died on November 13, 1780. He is buried at Trinity Church Cemetery in New York City. Although it was named for him, he was never in what would become Woodford County.

Gen. Marquis Calmes IV (1755–1834), a veteran of the Revolutionary War and the War of 1812, is credited with naming the town of Versailles. Calmes was a founder and trustee of the town when it was established in 1792 and chose the name reportedly to honor General Lafayette, with whom he served. Calmes received 1,000 acres in Woodford County for his Revolutionary War service. The property was located on Paynes Mill Road, where General Calmes is buried in a stone mausoleum that is listed in the National Register of Historic Places.

Woodford County, being located between the capital city of Frankfort and the early-settled city of Lexington, has played an important role in state government and politics. It has provided six Kentucky governors, more than any other county. This achievement is noted by a plaque on a boulder shaped like the state of Kentucky in Governors Park at Versailles City Hall. (Courtesy of Mike Timperman.)

GOVERNORS PARK
HONORING
GOVERNORS OF KENTUCKY FROM WOODFORD COUNTY

CHARLES SCOTT	1808-1812
JOHN J. CRITTENDEN	1848-1850
LUKE P. BLACKBURN	1879-1883
ALBERT B. CHANDLER	1935-1939 & 1955-1959
MARTHA L. COLLINS	1983-1987
BRERETON C. JONES	1991-1995

THIS BOULDER, ORIGINALLY SHAPED LIKE KENTUCKY, WAS CARRIED IN THE INAUGURAL PARADES OF A.B. CHANDLER AND WAS LABELED "WOODFORD, SOLID AS A ROCK FOR CHANDLER". IT REMAINED NEXT TO THE GOVERNOR'S MANSION FOR A NUMBER OF YEARS UNTIL IT WAS MOVED BACK TO VERSAILLES IN THE 1960'S.

ESTABLISHED 1997
CHARLES R. REED, MAYOR
COUNCIL MEMBERS

ROY BENSON	GEOFFREY REID	FRED SIEGELMAN
LUTHER BLAND, JR.	OWEN ROBERTS	MARY ELLEN BRADLEY

Edmund H. Taylor was a businessman who started in banking in Versailles before becoming involved in bourbon. He worked hard to improve the standards in the distilling industry and thus is often referred to as the "Father of the Modern Bourbon Industry." In Woodford County, he started the Old Taylor Distillery and had a farm that excelled in raising purebred cattle.

John J. Crittenden was born in 1786 in a cabin near Lexington Road. Crittenden attended the nearby Pisgah Academy before going to college and becoming a lawyer. He entered political life, being elected governor, US representative, and senator. He also served as attorney general in President Fillmore's cabinet. In 1860, he introduced the Crittenden Compromise in the Senate in a last minute effort to preserve the Union and avoid war. Crittenden died in 1863 and is buried in the Frankfort Cemetery.

Because Kentucky was a divided state during the Civil War, it has been said that neighbors fought against neighbors and relatives against relatives. The Buford family of Woodford County provides an example. John and Abraham Buford, first cousins, were both West Point graduates who went on to excel as cavalry commanders—just not for the same side. John Buford (right) was born in the Rose Hill section of Woodford County. He became a brigadier general of cavalry for the Union army and fought with distinction at Gettysburg. Buford's cavalry held off a superior number of Confederate troops, allowing the Union to secure the strategic high ground, which most military experts think was the key to the Union victory. He did not survive the war and is buried at West Point. Abraham Buford (below) also fought with distinction during the war and obtained the rank of brigadier general in the Confederate cavalry. He participated in many of the battles and cavalry raids in the western theater of the war. After the war, he returned to his Woodford County horse farm, Bosque Bonita, which is today Lane's End farm on Midway Road.

47

One of the more notable citizens of Woodford County was Albert Benjamin "Happy" Chandler Sr. Although born in Henderson County, Chandler lived most of his life in Woodford County. He attended Transylvania College, where he was an outstanding athlete, playing basketball, baseball, and football. After graduating from the University of Kentucky law school, Chandler opened a law practice in Versailles. He soon became involved in politics and had a very successful public career, serving as two-time governor of Kentucky, lieutenant governor, and US senator. He also served as the commissioner of Major League Baseball from 1945 to 1951. However, all of that was in the future when the photograph below was taken in the 1920s. Here, he is just a young high school basketball coach with his Versailles High School team.

Josephine Henry (1846–1928) lived in Versailles and was a teacher, social reformer, and leading advocate for women's suffrage. She was instrumental in the passage by the Kentucky legislature of the 1894 Married Woman's Property Act. Her former home on Montgomery Avenue is on the National Votes for Women Trail and is designated by a historical marker. Henry is buried in the Versailles Cemetery.

The *Woodford Sun* newspaper has been published since 1869. Part of that success is due to the man shown here, Daniel M. Bowmar Jr. Due to the ill health of their father, who was the publisher of the *Sun*, brothers Daniel Jr. and Aitcheson took over publishing and editing the newspaper in 1885 when they were only teenagers. Daniel M. Bowmar Jr. continued in that capacity until his death 57 years later in 1942.

This 1890 photograph shows some of the businessmen of Woodford County. The purpose of their meeting is not known. From left to right are (first row) S.L. Pinkerton, D.T. Edwards, Field McLeod, W.O. Davis, and James S. Stevens; (second row) D.L. Thornton, R.H. Gray, J.C. Bailey, Thomas Porter, L.H. Parrish, and R.H. Stout; (third row) D.W. Edwards, W.S. Barbour, and E.M. Wallace.

This 1947 photograph shows various city and county officials posing on the steps of the courthouse. From left to right are Marshall Dawson, Snooks Beasley, Frank Lathren, Matt Blackard, John Gray, Will Dozier, D.L. Thornton, and George McGohon. Blackard served as the county judge/executive from the late 1930s through the 1970s.

Four

CHURCHES

When settlers moved to what would become Woodford County, they did not leave their spirituality behind. Establishing churches and other places of worship seems to have been a priority with them. Consequently, various congregations are some of the oldest institutions in the county. While some have modern church buildings, others continue to worship in churches that are well over 100 years old and in some cases are the original buildings.

Early residents showed great flexibility in their desire for a spiritual life. If there were not enough members of a given denomination to support building a church, they would combine with other denominations to build a "union" or "republic" church. The different denominations would then use the church on a rotating basis, with each minister taking turns conducting services on Sunday. The Old Stone Church in Millville was such a church. Some members would attend services regularly, even though their minister may not have been preaching on any given Sunday.

Early on, there were an amazing number of churches despite the rural nature of most of the county. This was due mainly to the difficulty of travel. For example, in the late 1800s, there were Presbyterian churches at Nonesuch, Elm Corner, Troy, and just across the Jessamine County line at Ebenezer. With improvements in transportation, it was no longer necessary to have numerous churches in a small area, so the various churches were merged into the one at Troy.

Presented in this chapter is a sampling of the various churches that have existed in Woodford County. Most are still going strong, but some are no more than memories. While this collection of photographs covers several churches, it is not complete. If a particular church building is not included, it does not mean it was not worthy of inclusion but rather that it was not in the historical society's collection or was otherwise not available.

The Big Spring Baptist Meeting House was constructed for a Baptist congregation in 1819 at 121 Rose Hill Avenue in Versailles. Its preacher was Jacob Creath, an outstanding speaker who was admired by the great orator Henry Clay. The church declined after a large part of its congregation, including its minister, converted to the Christian Church denomination and went on to form the First Christian Church of Versailles (see page 60). The building ceased being used as a church in the 1850s and over the decades has been used for a variety of purposes. Today, it is the home of the Woodford County Historical Society.

The Forks of Elkhorn Baptist congregation was formed in 1788 in Franklin County. The church moved to Woodford County in 1866 when it took over the Harmony Presbyterian Church building. In 1912, it moved to Duckers to be near a train depot, and constructed this building. The church was destroyed in a 1943 fire. The church's current location is across the road from its original site.

The Grassy Springs Church, also known as Hopewell, was organized in 1798 near what today is Grassy Spring Pike. Originally a Baptist congregation, it converted to the Christian denomination in 1830. This c. 1893–1895 photograph shows the third building of the congregation, constructed in 1869. The church was discontinued in the 1940s, and most members transferred to the Millville Christian Church. This building was razed shortly thereafter.

This attractive wood-frame building was the first home of the Millville Baptist Church, built in 1891. It was in the center of Millville and served until 1952, when the congregation erected its current brick building nearby. This photograph was taken around 1900. The wooden rail in front of the stone fence was no doubt to tie up horses.

This 1917 photograph shows members of the Mortonsville Christian Church on a church picnic. The location is believed to have been an old log cabin near where Sellers Mill Road crosses Tanner Creek. The church was one of three in the community of Mortonsville.

This undated photograph shows the abandoned building of what was the first church in Millville. It was built in 1830 and was called the Old Stone Church or Glens Creek Republican Meeting House. This was an example of where there were not enough members of one denomination to support building a church. In such situations, members of different denominations would pool their resources and build a church that they would take turns using. It was said that this church had a large scroll of white cotton on which the words of hymns were written. After the Baptist and Christian congregations built their own churches in Millville, there were not enough remaining members to support the church, and it was abandoned around 1896. Having served three generations of worshippers, the church was taken down and its stone used for other purposes.

The first church in the community of Pinckard was a nondenominational church built in the early 1900s. It closed but reopened in the 1930s as a mission of the Mount Pleasant Baptist Church of Keene, Jessamine County. It became independent of Mount Pleasant in 1936 and has thrived ever since. This undated photograph shows members in front of the frame church that was used prior to its current brick building.

The Troy Presbyterian Church has been a landmark on Troy Pike (Route 33) in southern Woodford County since 1875. The church was organized in 1872 when two area Presbyterian churches that dated to the late 1700s merged. This photograph was taken in 1887. The church remains an active congregation whose fellowship hall is often used for community events.

The Versailles United Methodist Church congregation was formed in the early 1800s. Its first known permanent building was constructed in 1824 at the corner of Park and Green Streets. After the congregation outgrew the first building, the structure at right was built on Court Street in 1851. This building was used until 1922, when it was replaced with the one below. This 1949 view looks nothing like the existing building at the site. This is because in 1965 a new facade replaced the old one, a 109-foot steeple was added, and the building was painted white. It is no longer used as a church after the congregation moved to a larger building on Lexington Road. The building partially visible at left below was the old county jail.

This 1934 photograph of the Pisgah Presbyterian Church shows that it has changed very little in the last 85 years. It has long been a historic landmark on the Pisgah Pike in eastern Woodford County near the Fayette County line. The church was founded in 1784, with the current building constructed in 1812. The building was remodeled in 1868, which gave the church its current appearance. In the late 1700s, the grounds were also the site of the Kentucky Academy, which in 1798 merged with what would become Transylvania University in Lexington. Several prominent Woodford County residents were members of the church, and some are buried in its cemetery. It remains an active congregation today.

The building for St. Leo Catholic Church, at 238 North Main Street in Versailles, was dedicated on October 15, 1893. For the first 30 years of its existence, the church was a mission parish served by the pastor from St. Luke Church in Nicholasville. In 1924, the Covington Diocese appointed the first resident pastor for St. Leo, and it became an independent parish. In 1926, St. Leo School opened across Main Street from the church. The Woodford County Catholic community continued to grow to the extent that it became necessary to have Sunday mass in the school gym across the street. St. Leo moved to its current location on Huntertown Road in 1989, and this building subsequently became home to various private businesses over the years. The house to the left of the church served as the residence for the priest assigned to the parish.

The First Christian Church of Versailles, at 160 Lexington Street, is one of Woodford County's oldest active congregations. It was formed in 1830 out of a Baptist congregation that met at the Big Spring Baptist Meeting House on Rose Hill Avenue (see page 52). This is the current sanctuary, which was built in 1853. The photograph is from the 1940s.

The Versailles Baptist Church has had a presence at the northeast corner of North Main and Green Streets in downtown Versailles since 1846, having been organized in 1842. This 1940s photograph shows its second building, constructed in 1884 and remodeled in 1928. It was used until 1968, when it was replaced by the current building.

Five

TRANSPORTATION

A few years ago, a tour guide at the Woodford Reserve Distillery (where distilling began in 1812) related that a person on one of his tours asked, "Why was this distillery built so far from the interstate?" The question, as naïve as it was, does illustrate the tendency to think that roads and modes of transportation have not changed. Of course, just the opposite is true.

Today, no cargo or passengers are transported on the portion of the Kentucky River that borders Woodford County, but this was not always the case. Beginning pretty much with the settlement of the area, the river was used to float products downstream. Later, steamboats transported freight and passengers up and down the river. They even brought entertainment to residents living along the river in the form of showboats that would dock at the various landings.

By the early 1900s, steamboat traffic began to wane due to competition from railroads. A map sketched by *Woodford Sun* editor Dan Bowmar Jr. in 1921 showed the three railroad lines that ran through Versailles, which was served by as many as 14 trains a day. Today, the county has no passenger rail service and limited freight service.

While relatively early roads connected various sections of the county, they were nothing like the paved and well-maintained roads taken for granted today. Many were maintained by private companies, which collected tolls from those using them. Having to stop and pay the fees at the tollhouses that dotted the county was the bane of travelers until the county government bought out the last toll road in 1896.

The photographs in this chapter provide a look at these methods of transportation over the decades and what they meant to Woodford County.

The Kentucky River makes up Woodford County's southern and western border. The county has 40 miles of shoreline on the river, running from US Army Corps of Engineers river mile 72 to river mile 112. With the first bridge for vehicular traffic along this portion of the river not being built until 1932, ferries sprang up to transport residents across the river. Not surprisingly, today no less than seven roads in the western part of the county still have the word "ferry" in their name. Shown above around the 1930s is the ferry at Clifton (also known as Woodford Landing). Below is the ferry at Mundy's Landing (also known as Shawnee Run Ferry) in the early 1900s. The ferry at Mundy's Landing was closed in 1927.

The interurban was an electric trolley that connected Versailles with Lexington and Frankfort from 1906 until 1934. The route through Versailles came down Lexington Road, made a right onto Main Street, and then headed out Frankfort Road. Traces of the former track can still be seen on the south side of Route 60 between Versailles and Frankfort. When the company ceased operating in 1934, the rails were taken up and sent to Knott County for use on a railroad serving the area's coal mines. The c. 1920 photograph above shows one of the cars and its crew. The photograph below shows an interurban track crew with the tools of their trade. (Above, courtesy of Nostalgia Station Toy and Train Museum.)

This incredible photograph shows a brand-new Blackburn Bridge across the Kentucky River, not yet open to traffic. It carries Tyrone Pike (Route 62) between Woodford and Anderson Counties. It was completed in 1932 by the Virginia Bridge and Iron Company. It is of the somewhat rare S-bridge design with a curve at each end. The bridge is 1,256 feet in length and is believed to be the only three-span S-bridge in the United States. This view is from the Anderson County side

looking east into Woodford County. The bridge was named for Joseph Blackburn (1838–1918), who was born near Spring Station in Woodford County. After serving in the Confederate army, he returned to Woodford County, where he opened a law practice. He was elected to the US Congress, serving terms both as a representative and a senator. In 1907, he was appointed by Pres. Theodore Roosevelt to serve as governor of the Panama Canal Zone.

The Woodford County Historical Society's files identify this as possibly the first motorcar in the county. The photograph is from around 1903. The young girl in the rear seat is Natalie Brother. She is with her mother and father, Hattie Harris Brother and Hunter Brother. A 1904 article in the *Woodford Sun* reported that young Natalie, as an eight-year-old, drove the car with great skill and was known as the "youngest chauffeur in the county." Considerable driving skill was no doubt required to deal with some of the early-20th-century county roads.

The photograph above shows the imposing length and height of Young's High Bridge, a railroad bridge that spans the Kentucky River between Anderson County and Woodford County at Tyrone. It opened in 1889 and was built to carry traffic of the Louisville Southern Railroad. It was named for William Bennett Young, a native of Nicholasville, Kentucky, who became a prominent attorney known for his philanthropic work. He was also an officer of the Louisville Southern Railroad. At 283 feet high and with a span of 1,659 feet, it was and remains an impressive sight and engineering feat. The last regular passenger train crossed the bridge in 1937, but it remained in service for freight traffic until the 1980s. In recent years, it has occasionally been used for bungee jumping. The photograph below shows the completion and dedication of the bridge in 1889. (Both, courtesy of Bluegrass Railroad Museum Inc.)

The Milner depot was on the Southern Railway approximately five miles west of Versailles and two miles east of Young's Railroad Bridge, shown on the preceding page. As can be seen on the "Milner" sign at the top of the building, it was located 18.1 miles west of Lexington and 69.2 miles east of Louisville. An interesting group of individuals of all ages have turned out to have their photograph taken, probably around 1900. Passenger traffic on the line was discontinued in 1937, and the depot was demolished in the 1940s. However, the tracks that pass by the site of the former depot are used today by the Bluegrass Railroad Museum's excursion train. (Courtesy of Bluegrass Railroad Museum Inc.)

Shown here sometime around 1900 is the Versailles depot of the Southern Railway, originally the Louisville Southern Railway. The depot was used until 1937, when passenger service was discontinued, although the line continued to be used until the 1980s for freight trains. The building still exists, having been moved to front on Frankfort Street, and today houses a restaurant.

This building was the Spring Station freight depot, a stop on the L&N Railroad between Duckers and Midway. Spring Station was one of the original stops on the Lexington & Ohio Railroad when it commenced operations in 1833. It was originally referred to as Big Spring on early railroad maps. This depot remained in operation until sometime in the 1950s. The building still sits, abandoned, along the railroad tracks.

The town of Midway grew up around the railroad. The first train to serve the town was on the Lexington & Ohio line in 1833. The L&N Railroad acquired that line in 1881. The L&N depot, shown in the 1950s, was built sometime before 1900. The last train stopped here on December 5, 1966. In 1863, Confederate general John Hunt Morgan and his cavalry troops occupied the town. The troops took control of the earlier depot at this location. Morgan's telegraph operator then proceeded to send out bogus orders to Union troops, which created much confusion and delayed their response. The depot shown no longer exists. (Courtesy of Nostalgia Station Toy and Train Museum.)

Lida and Victor Crain, with their young daughter Frances, are shown waiting at the Versailles L&N depot in the 1920s. Victor Crain worked 47 years for the *Woodford Sun*, primarily as the paper's printing plant foreman. He also served on the Versailles City Council. Lida Crain lived to be one of Woodford County's oldest residents, passing away in 1999 at the age of 105. (Courtesy of Nostalgia Station Toy and Train Museum.)

The repurposing of railroad depots after rail service has terminated is illustrated by this photograph from the 1940s. After the L&N passenger depot in Versailles closed in 1932, it was used for various other purposes, including by the Versailles Pentecostal Church of God. Here, a group of children dressed for Sunday services are having their photograph taken on what was the platform of the depot. (Courtesy of Nostalgia Station Toy and Train Museum.)

Originally, many county roads were maintained by private companies that charged travelers a toll for using them, and were usually referred to as turnpikes. At one time, all of the roads into Versailles were subject to tolls. Road operators installed tollhouses with wooden poles that could be raised and lowered to enforce the tolls. This 1870s photograph shows the tollhouse at Troy with the gate pole to the right. This was at the busy intersection of today's Route 33 and the Troy-Keene Road, where the tollhouse could charge for travel on both roads. Given the amount of traffic on these two important roads, the turnpike company no doubt did a thriving business.

Woodford County had the distinction of being the corporate home of one of the country's largest railroads, the Southern Pacific Railroad Company. However, not one mile of the company's track was located in the state. Southern Pacific was based here solely to take advantage of Kentucky's favorable tax rates. The railroad was originally located in Jefferson County, Kentucky, until Lt. Gov. Happy Chandler convinced the company to move to Spring Station in 1932. Its activities in the county were largely limited to its annual meeting. The corporate office shown above was built in 1939 at Spring Station and still exists as a private home. The photograph below shows the shareholders at one of the meetings. A lawsuit in 1946 changed how railroad property was assessed, greatly reducing the tax benefit. As a result, the railroad left the county the following year.

At the turn of the 20th century, steamboats on the Kentucky River were an important method of transportation for both freight and passengers, as illustrated by this photograph. Passengers wait to board as cargo is being loaded. The location of this particular landing in Woodford County is not positively identified, but it is believed to be Mundy's Landing in the southern part of the county. In addition to hauling freight and passengers, showboats would also come up the river and tie up along the banks to offer entertainment to local residents. Steamboat traffic on the river began to wane in the early 1900s due to the competition from railroads.

Six
BUSINESS ESTABLISHMENTS

Today, chambers of commerce and similar organizations encourage citizens to "shop local" to support hometown businesses. In the 1800s and a large part of the 1900s, residents of Woodford County did just that, not by choice but out of necessity. Given the methods of travel and, in some cases, less than ideal roads, going to a larger town or city to purchase goods and services was not practical. Additionally, some services needed to be procured close to where one lived, such as those provided by blacksmiths, sawmills, and gristmills.

Thus there was a demand for goods and services to be provided locally, and it was met by local merchants, craftsmen, and other service providers. The photographs in this and the following chapter will show some of the business establishments that met the needs of Woodford County residents. They were mainly located in the county seat of Versailles and in the town of Midway. However, the communities previously discussed, such as Mortonsville, Clifton, Troy, and Millville, all had their share of retail businesses and shops.

S. Pelosi Restaurant and Confectionery was located at 110 Main Street in Versailles. It sold candy, nuts, fruit, vegetables, and other foods. These photographs were taken before 1910. At left, owner Salvatore Pelosi is standing second from the left; his wife, Cecelia, is beside him. Below is the interior of the business. From left to right are Harry Taylor, Tim McCarty, and Salvatore Pelosi. Taylor appears to be enjoying a drink made from the ingredients on the counter in front of him. Pelosi sold the business in 1915 to Victor Mucci, who ran it for the next 31 years.

This 1899 photograph shows the Wasson Drug Store, located in the Ballard Building on the northwest corner of Main and Court Streets. The drugstore operated from 1896 until about 1909, when the Woodford Bank & Trust Company took over the building. The building was replaced in 1926 and today is occupied by a bank. At left is John M. Wasson, and in the doorway is owner D. Edgar Wasson.

This building at 185 South Main Street in Versailles has been home to several different hardware stores. It was built in 1896 by John S. Minary. In the 1950s, it was Colyer Hardware, and from the late 1960s to the mid-1970s it was Your Hardware. It is shown here in 1914, when it was Minary Hardware. Like all good hardware stores, it has a sample of its wares out on the sidewalk.

This Texaco service station was on North Main Street where North Main Street Extension, Broadway, and North Main, Elm, and Frankfort Streets all meet. The 1944 photograph shows Doc Britton, an employee of Ward Robinson, who owned the station at that time. Over the years, the station had different owners, including Tommy Hendricks, Gene Green, John Tilghman, and George Roberts. It was torn down in the 1960s.

This c. 1930 photograph shows that Versailles had a taxi service with at least two cabs. This stand was at 143 Lexington Street. A substantial portion of business would have been passengers arriving at the various railroad depots in Versailles and nearby communities.

This drawing shows one of the earliest businesses in Versailles, Watkins Tavern. It was built in the 1790s at the southwest corner of Main and Court Streets, where the former Amsden bank building is today. It was owned and operated by Henry and Elizabeth Watkins. Elizabeth was Henry Clay's mother. The tavern was the site of a dinner in honor of General Lafayette's visit in 1825. It burned in 1886. (Drawing in Woodford County Historical Society files; courtesy of Ron Wells.)

The O'Neal House, shown here in 1912, was built in 1881 at 112 North Main Street in Versailles. It was the first building in town constructed specifically to serve as a hotel and contained 26 rooms. It had a reputation for comfortable accommodations and good food for its guests. The building is still in use, having been remodeled into apartments in 1991.

This c. 1910 photograph shows "Uncle" John T. Gatrell and Bab Gatrell in front of William Arthur Gatrell's grocery in Midway. The store was on the north side of Railroad Street. The man at far left is unidentified. The grocery store was burned in the 1915 fire that destroyed the entire Collins Building block in Midway.

There was no business more important to a farming community than the blacksmith. The local blacksmith made horseshoes, wagon wheel rims, and various farm implements in addition to repairing broken items. Shown here is Jesse Bain's blacksmith shop, which operated in Midway from 1928 until 1951.

Troy is another example of a village that once had businesses but no longer does. This is the blacksmith shop of W.D. Herod, which operated from 1912 to 1919. As shown by the sign, it took advantage of the traffic on the busy road that ran through Troy (today's Route 33) by offering horseshoeing and rubber tires. The tires were probably for both carriages and automobiles.

This c. 1915 photograph is of the Seals Store in Troy, at the intersection of today's Route 33 and Troy-Keene Road. From left to right are (first row) Charlie Black and Frank Singleton; (second row) Hudson Seal, Jim Deeringer, Henry Bruce Seal, John Matt Deeringer, Wallace Johnson, and Dick Kincaid. Although Seals closed many years ago, a store building is still located at the intersection.

This country store was located in Nonesuch in southern Woodford County. It has the typical appearance of a store found out in the county during much of the early and mid-1900s. It is a small frame building with plenty of advertising signs. The store was at the intersection of Cummins Ferry Road and Ford's Mill Road. The square object on the porch was a tank containing kerosene for sale to customers. These small stores filled an important niche in that local residents could get staples without having to travel to Versailles, Midway, or other towns. Although today Nonesuch has a general store near where this store was located, most of the county's country stores are long gone.

The John G. Manuel Store stood for many years in the community of Mortonsville. The owner, Manuel, lived in Mortonsville not far from the store. It was in business by at least 1877, since the store was shown on the county map of that date. It was later owned by John Davis, then George Benjamin Wilson, and then Everett Mitchell. The building burned down in the 1970s.

This photograph was labeled in the Woodford County Historical Society's files as the Earl Clough store. However, there are no records indicating that Clough, who worked on clocks, owned an automobile parts store in Versailles. The shelves contain headlights, horns, cans of oil, and other car parts. A windshield can be seen at center, behind the cabinet with the small drawers.

These before-and-after images of the Farmers Bank of Mortonsville tell the story of many of Woodford County's small communities and their businesses. The bank opened on December 17, 1906, in the new building shown in the drawing above. The *Woodford Sun* reported that the directors of the new bank were all "successful and conservative business men of the highest standing in the community and whose connection with the institution give it strength and solidity." Despite this solid foundation, there was not enough business for the bank to be profitable. The bank ceased operations after 22 years when, in 1928, it was absorbed by the Amsden Bank of Versailles and this building was closed. As the various businesses in Mortonsville closed, their former buildings fell into disrepair and eventually were taken down. The abandoned bank building shown below was demolished sometime after 2000.

Chapman's Grocery Store was located at Elm Corner, approximately seven miles south of Versailles at the intersection of Route 33, Ford's Mill Road, and Elm Corner Road. This 1949 photograph also shows the former Elm Corner schoolhouse on the right. All that remains of the store is some of the pavement, but the school building has been converted to a private residence.

This is a 1924 photograph of the interior of the Prillman Store on Main Street in Versailles. The man is Bob Montgomery, and the woman standing at center behind the counter is Mary Schlanks. It is not known when the store closed.

One can almost smell the ink from this photograph of the *Woodford Sun* newspaper office in 1914. The *Sun*, published since 1869, is one of the state's oldest newspapers. Shown here is the printing room of the newspaper. From left to right are Homer Kleim, Victor Crain, and *Sun* owner and publisher Daniel Bowmar. Daniel Bowmar and his brother Aitchison A. were the longtime publishers of the newspaper. The belt attached to the overhead wheel and shaft provided the power to operate the press.

Shown here in the 1920s is the inside of the Farmer's Union Flour Mill with part of its workforce. Established in 1913, the mill was located in the town of Versailles on North Main Street Extension. The mill used a steam engine with a coal-fired boiler as its power source. After the Farmer's Union was dissolved, it was subsequently owned by C.A. Howard, Henry Broderson, and Walter Crews. The mill closed in the early 1960s, when it was owned by the Weisenberger family (see page 94). After the mill business closed, the building was demolished in the mid-1960s. The darker sacks to the right of the workers have the label "Mill Feed" with the date 1923.

Seven
Farms, Distilleries, and Other Industries

This chapter continues with photographs of Woodford County businesses and commercial activities, with an emphasis on farming and manufacturing interests. Woodford County, being in the heart of the fertile Inner Bluegrass region, has always been an agricultural community. The county early on was known for its livestock, especially cattle and Thoroughbred horses. Many farms grew hemp and tobacco as their primary cash crops. They also grew wheat, oats, and other grains to feed themselves and their animals. Corn likewise was grown for feed and also to make bourbon whiskey.

In addition to the many farms and plantations in the county, there were the various businesses necessary to support an agricultural economy. Gristmills that ground the grains and distilleries that turned corn into bourbon dotted the county.

These photographs are a sample of the various farming and industrial pursuits at different times from the mid-1800s through the 1940s.

The distilled product that would become known as bourbon whiskey was first made in central Kentucky. Woodford County had its share of distilleries, beginning in the early 1800s and continuing to this day. Shown here is the Old Taylor Distillery in Millville, near the Franklin County line. The distillery was started in 1887 by Edmund H. Taylor (see page 46), a pioneer in the bourbon industry who worked to improve the quality of the product. Old Taylor Distillery soon became iconic for the Kentucky bourbon industry, primarily because of its impressive buildings and grounds. Its main office, shown here, was built as a stone castle, complete with turrets. The photograph below shows it under construction in 1911.

Part of Edmund Taylor's vision for his distillery was that, in addition to being a manufacturing plant where whiskey was produced, it would be a tourist attraction that folks would want to visit. Accordingly, the grounds were beautifully landscaped. Included within the grounds was a sunken garden, shown above. The men in the photograph below, taken in 1915, are enjoying a walk in the garden, which is still in existence on the grounds, having been restored by the current operator of the distillery. The man in the dark suit on the right is Edmund Taylor's son, Kenner Taylor.

The late 1800s photograph above shows some of the production workers at the Old Taylor Distillery. Today, the making of bourbon has been automated so that the amount of manual labor has been greatly reduced. That was not the case at the time these photographs were taken. Given the several steps of making fine bourbon, distilling was a labor-intensive activity. It required hard manual labor to unload grains, transfer the liquids after fermentation, shovel coal for the steam boilers, and handle the heavy barrels of bourbon. The small child sitting on the dock at the left below was no doubt a worker's daughter. The photograph below shows the office staff and part of the production crew.

After bourbon goes into the barrel, it spends several years aging in warehouses. Warehouses at many distilleries are often of basic, utilitarian design, some being plain buildings covered with tin siding—but not at the Old Taylor Distillery. Note how this brick warehouse also has the castle motif at the top of the tower.

This postcard shows the bottling line at the Old Taylor Distillery. The interiors of the Old Taylor buildings apparently were given as much attention to detail as the landscaping and exteriors. The bottling room has potted plants, a fountain, and decorative light fixtures.

Weisenberger Mill, located on South Elkhorn Creek three miles east of Midway, has been in the Weisenberger family since 1865. That year, August Weisenberger bought an existing mill at the site, and the business has continued for six generations. Today, the mill provides a number of consumer products. Although it has a Midway address, the mill building itself sits on the Scott County side of the creek. This is the view looking from Woodford County. Stone from the original mill was used for the concrete in the construction of this building in 1913. The one-horse wagon below was one of the company's delivery vehicles used in the early 1900s.

A mill was established on Grier's Creek in central western Woodford County by Joel Dupuy in the 1790s. The mill was approximately one mile down Grier's Creek Road from its intersection with Scott's Ferry Road. The mill was purchased by Thomas Dean in the mid-1800s and then by Squire Willis in 1878, although it sometimes continued to be referred to as the Old Dupuy Mill. The building shown in this 1902 photograph is a later mill built at the site, although some of the stonework is from the original 1790s mill.

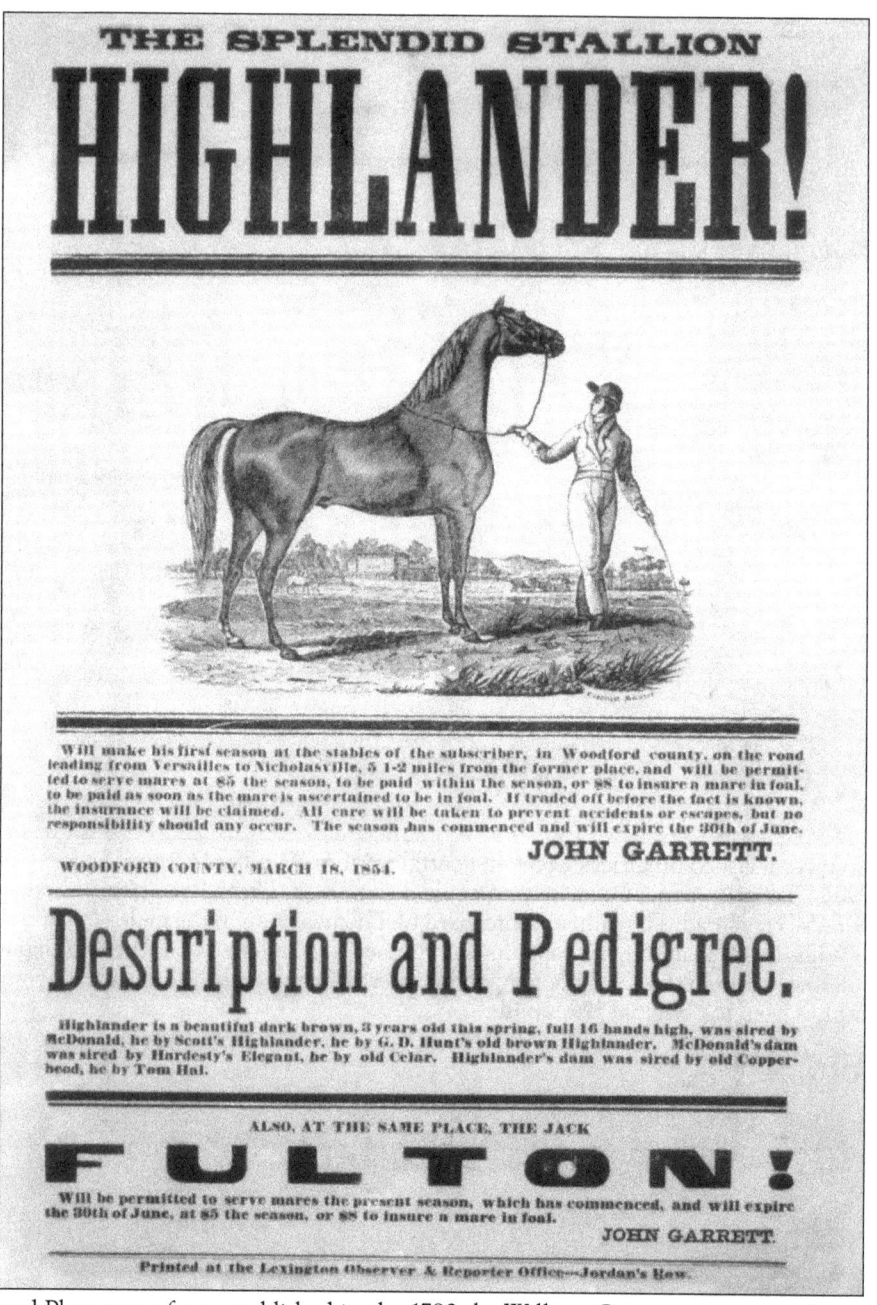

Highland Place was a farm established in the 1780s by William Garrett approximately six miles south of Versailles near the intersection of Nicholasville Pike (Route 169) and Shannon Run Road. The farm was in the Garrett family for several generations and was known for its excellent horse bloodlines. The Richmond, Nicholasville, Irvine & Beattyville Railroad, known as the "Riney-B" (later the L&N), had a stop on the property that was referred to as Fort Garrett. This flyer from March 1854 is a notice by William's son, John Garrett, that the farm's leading stallion, Highlander, and the jack (male donkey) Fulton were available for breeding. The donkey would have been bred to female horses to produce mules. Today's Thoroughbred breeders would be amazed at the $5 and $8 stud fees advertised.

Bourbon has been made at this site on the Grassy Creek branch of Glenn's Creek near Millville since 1812. That year, Elijah Pepper moved his distillery from downtown Versailles to this site because the two springs here provided a better source of water. In the 1830s, the distillery's operation was taken over by Elijah's son, Oscar, and it became known as the Old Oscar Pepper Distillery. Oscar Pepper hired James Crow as the master distiller. Crow, a chemist by training, is credited with bringing the scientific process to the making of bourbon whiskey at this location. US senator Henry Clay from Lexington was said to be particularly fond of the bourbon made here. He was known to occasionally take a barrel of it to Washington, DC, to, in Clay's words, "lubricate the wheels of government." After Oscar Pepper died, it became the Labrot & Graham Distillery, shown here in the 1880s. Today it is the Woodford Reserve Distillery and is a very popular stop on the Kentucky Bourbon Trail.

These 1883 photographs show workers at the Labrot & Graham Distillery. The photograph above shows production workers posing outside of the distillery building. Some are holding tools used in the distilling business. The sign on the wall above the workers has the name "Labrot & Graham" and the number 52, which was the federal government registration number for this distillery. Today, the Woodford Reserve Distillery at the site has the same registration number. The photograph below was taken in the bottling room, where the finished product was bottled and packed in boxes. All of the women are in uniform.

These typical 1920s farming scenes were taken on the farm of Field McLeod (1867–1947), a prominent attorney and citizen in Versailles. Judge McLeod owned two farms in the county: 98 acres near Faywood and 380 acres near Milner. After his death, the farms were placed in trust to provide income for McLeod's wife and sister and were eventually given for the benefit of the Cleveland Home in Versailles. The individual operating the equipment above and standing fourth from left below has been identified as Jim Curry. The photograph above shows a binder, which was used to cut small grains (such as wheat) and bind it into bundles. The bundles would then be placed in shocks.

This large piece of equipment was a portable steam engine used to supply power to farm equipment, most likely in this case a threshing machine. The steam engine traveled from farm to farm at harvest time. The large leather belt provided power to whatever piece of equipment it was attached to. This photograph was taken on one of the McLeod farms along with the photographs on the preceding page.

Hemp was an important crop in Woodford County prior to the Civil War. Hemp fiber was used for making rope, coarse cloth, and bagging for cotton bales. The crop had a revival in the early 1940s to support the country's war efforts in World War II. Shown here are shocks of hemp in Woodford County around 1940. This hemp has been cut and dried and is ready to have the fiber separated from the stalk.

In the 1980s, the US National Park Service conducted a property survey known as the Historic America Engineering Record. It identified the former Guyn family mill and related buildings off of Paul's Mill Road in southern Woodford County as an excellent example of a 19th-century rural industrial complex. The complex consisted of a sawmill, gristmill, blacksmiths shop, general store, and other buildings. The gristmill was constructed in the 1870s and used steam, rather than water, for its power source. Although this photograph was taken in the 1970s, it shows the building essentially as it was during the time it operated. The building has since been renovated and is being used as commercial space. The former sawmill and blacksmith shop still exist on the property, which is privately owned and not open to the public. (Courtesy of the Library of Congress.)

The tobacco harvest, shown here, has long been a fall ritual in central Kentucky. In this scene, the tobacco plants have been cut and placed on sticks that are being loaded on the wagon. The plants will be hung in a barn to dry for several months before being taken to market. Today, the amount of tobacco grown in Woodford County has been greatly reduced, but it is still harvested the same way.

This classic Bluegrass image was made in 1894 at Sunny Slope Farm, on Aiken Road off Midway Road. Established in the 1780s, the farm was a successful horse, cattle, hemp, and tobacco operation and was home to six generations of the Shipp family. The family home in the background was built in 1820. The farm was originally known as Lovedale.

The Harper family had much success in the racing world in the second half of the 19th century from their farm near Midway. Shown here are two racehorses that were part of that success. Above is the great racer Longfellow with its owner John Harper. Longfellow was born in 1867 and out of 17 starts had 13 wins and 3 second places. Below is perhaps an even greater racer, Ten Broeck. Ten Broeck was foaled in 1872 and was very successful on the track. Out of 30 starts, he had 23 wins, 3 second places, and 1 third place.

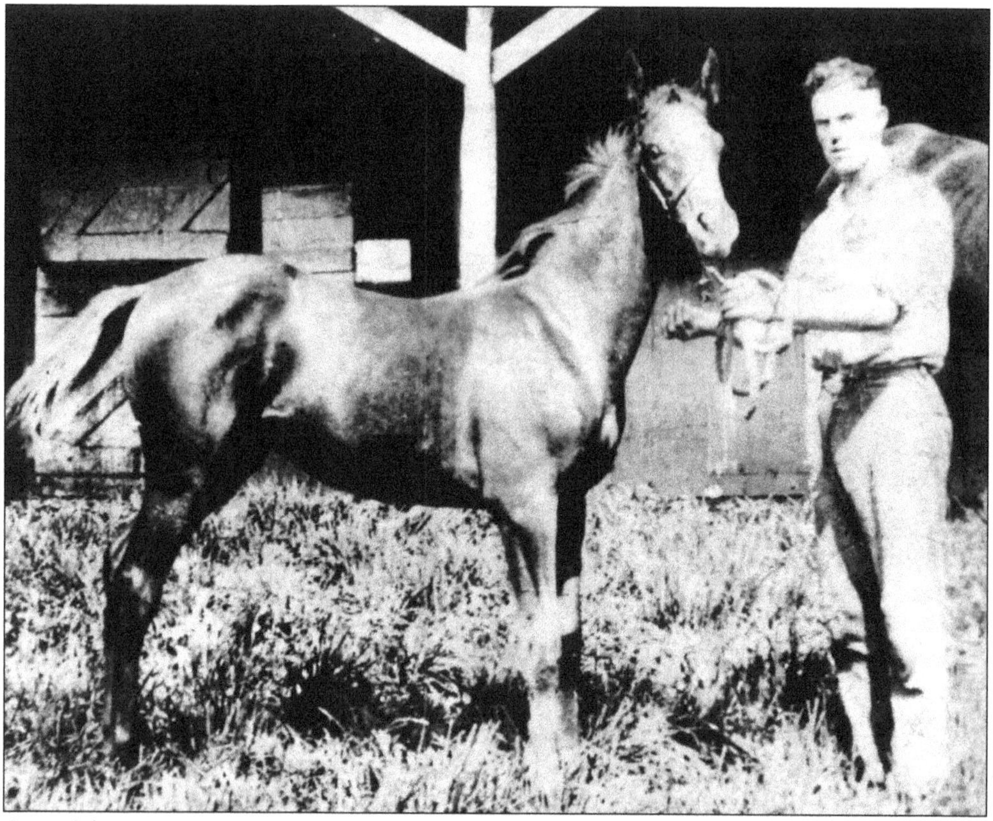

One of the greatest racehorses of all time was Man of War, shown here as a weanling. Although foaled in Fayette County, Man of War had a Woodford County connection. Shown with the horse in 1917 is J. Bryan Martin (1899–1978) of Midway. Martin was Man of War's first trainer and the first person to ride the famous horse. This is the earliest known photograph of Man of War. (Courtesy of Nicholas Martin.)

The Hereford bull Woodford was a world champion whose offspring were the foundation of many of the world's great Hereford herds. He was purchased by E.H. Taylor (see page 46) in the early 1900s for the then-incredible sum of $12,500 for his Hereford cattle farm in northern Woodford County. Sadly, the great bull died in a barn fire in 1918.

Eight

DAILY LIFE

Many of the photographs in the Woodford County Historical Society's collection shown in the previous chapters focused primarily on structures and things. These included churches, schools, depots, mills, distilleries, and other buildings. Additionally, there were government buildings, street scenes, railroads, bridges, and roads. There were also images of people, including well-known or famous individuals and groups formally posing for the camera.

The society also has photographs of ordinary people doing everyday things, whether it was work, leisure, or socializing. Most of these are of individuals who took time from what they were doing to pose for the camera. However, some are candid, taken while the subjects were just going about what they were doing. This chapter presents a selection of these, showing, as the chapter title states, their daily lives. It is these photographs that perhaps give the best insight into what life was like in Woodford County from the mid-1800s to 1950.

These young men are posing at the bridge across Tanner's Creek in the community of Mortonsville. The photograph was taken looking west on Delaney Ferry Road. The building to the right was a blacksmith shop. Baseball appears to have been a popular pastime for the village's youths.

Started in 1935 to help relieve unemployment during the Great Depression, the Works Progress Administration (WPA) provided training in many different arts and trades. Shown here around 1939 is the Woodford County WPA Sewing Unit, where participants learned to sew and make clothing items that could be sold. The supervisor, standing in the back, is Ida Mae Baker. This photograph was taken in the Woodford County Courthouse, where the group met.

Versailles Fair, Aug. 7, 8 and 9, 1912

"BLUE BLOODS"

The Woodford County Fair began in 1892, when a fair association was formed and purchased land on Big Sink Pike (where Crossfield Drive is today). That same year, the association constructed a large grandstand for horse-related events. County fairs took place at this location until the grandstand was lost in a fire. As shown in this postcard, horses were a big part of the fair. The postcard from the 1912 fair, showing a young lady holding the two horses, has the caption "Blue Bloods," which one has to assume was intended to refer to both the person and the horses. The Woodford County Fair is still held each June at Beasley Road off of Tyrone Pike (Route 62).

This 1918 image shows the Versailles Fire Department with the first fire truck (as opposed to a horse-drawn wagon). The man standing on the truck is Ed Dozier. The station was on Green Street, although its exact address could not be identified.

The only thing better than going to a farmer's market to get fresh produce is having the farmer deliver it. That was the case with the man in this undated photograph. James R. Adams (1863–1937) sold vegetables from his farm in Woodford County from his mule-drawn wagon. He is buried in the Versailles Cemetery.

John Cleveland was a successful farmer in southern Woodford County. Upon his death in 1869, his will provided that his estate be used for the "educating, feeding, and clothing of poor orphan females of the state." As a result, the Cleveland Orphan Home was formed in 1870 and continued as a residential facility in various formats until 2005. The c. 1905 photograph above shows residents standing in front of the building, which was located at the intersection of Park and Green Streets in Versailles. The photograph below shows the home's 1938 Christmas dinner, which was held at a local restaurant.

This c. 1890 photograph shows the family of Ernest and Amelia Huffman, who emigrated from Germany in 1882. The three children shown—from left to right, Rosa, Ernestine, and Max—were all born in this country. The man on the right near the porch is unidentified. The family is shown at Canewood, the farm of Bernard Gratz on the southeastern corner of the intersection of Old Frankfort Pike and Steele Road.

One thing that has not changed over the decades is the relationship between children and their pets. Shown here in 1911 is Jeannette Wasson (1899–1970) and her dog Bessie. Margaret Hall School (see page 37) is in the background.

This c. 1875 photograph shows that not every form of transportation of that period had wheels and was pulled by a fast horse. Sleds were sometimes used in the winter in lieu of wagons. The exact location of this photograph is unknown. The large house in the background might have been the Woodburn Plantation house (see page 118).

The Pisgah community boasted its own tennis club. In 1887, the Pisgah Presbyterian Church (see page 58) gave permission for clay tennis courts to be built on church property, and the club was formed shortly thereafter. Shown here are some of its members from 1935. From left to right are Jim Cox, Whitney Dunlap, Branham Dunlap, and Wilmore Garrett.

Edith Hunter Platt of Brooklyn, New York, is shown on the pony Bonnie Bell while visiting her grandmother Edith S. Hunter in 1899. The photograph was taken at Edith Hunter's farm, Dufont, on McCracken Pike. Dufont was known for its hospitality, and the Hunter family held many social gatherings there. Edith Platt died at a young age in 1902 due to health issues.

This smiling group is pictured in front of the Mortonsville Post Office sometime before it closed in 1921. Tom Wheat is driving the wagon, and from left to right are John B. Burles, Henderson "Jack" Owen, and D.G. Owen.

Camp Otonka was the summer camp of the Lexington Young Women's Christian Association. It was located on the Kentucky River in southern Woodford County, off McCowans Ferry Road. It consisted of a lodge (shown above), a large farmhouse used for dining, a dormitory, and 10 sleeping tents. Later, the tents and the dormitory were replaced with small cabins. A mess hall and other buildings were later added to the camp. Some young campers are shown sitting on the porch of the lodge during the summer of 1946. The photograph below shows some of the campers on an outing in 1939.

Clifton is a small community on the Kentucky River approximately seven miles west of Versailles. Established in the late 1700s, it was originally known as Woodford Landing. It became a thriving river town that was home to three distilleries, warehouses, a coal yard, a sawmill, and retail businesses. It later became known as Cicero and then finally as Clifton, taking its name from Thomas Railey's home on the cliffs overlooking the river. In the 1930s, Clifton became the site for summer camps on the river. Folks from all over central Kentucky flocked there to spend time and have holiday celebrations on the river. This interesting photograph shows two young women posing in the early 1900s at the two large stone chimneys that had been part of the Miller Distillery, which operated during the 1800s. One of the chimneys still exists in the backyard of a private residence.

Shown here is the vault where property and other records are kept in the Woodford County clerk's office in the courthouse. Employees are, at the front from left to right, Cora McDonald, Virginia House, and John Gray, the county clerk; the man in the back is unidentified. The desk seen here is currently at the Woodford County Historical Society.

This photograph was taken in 1908 inside the Cogar & Company building in Midway. From left to right are (first row) John Van de Graaf, James Cogar, Ike Parrish, and Charles Thomas; (second row) Will Cogar, Claude Rogers, unidentified, Dr. Ben Parrish, and J. Pat Haley. The Cogar building burned in 1912.

This is the Armistice Day parade in downtown Versailles celebrating the end of World War I. Fighting in the war ceased on November 11, 1918. A large crowd turned out, and there seems to be much excitement in the air. The parade is headed south on Main Street, as indicated by the Mastin Brothers store in the background. The shoe store was located on the east side of Main Street, two doors down from Lexington Street and across from the courthouse. Approximately 200 World War I soldiers and sailors marched in the parade. An article in the *Woodford Sun* at the time estimated the crowd at 3,000 and called the event "one of the biggest days in the history of Woodford County." Armistice Day is now celebrated as Veterans Day.

Nine
Distinctive Dwellings

No review of the historic photographs of any location would be complete without images of houses where local residents lived. The Woodford County Historical Society's collection of historic photographs of houses is not large, but it does include some of the notable and interesting homes in the county. Most still exist today as private homes. A few are long gone and exist only in memories or in photographs like those in this chapter. One, the Jack Jouett House, is publicly owned and open for tours. They represent a mix of design, size, and luxury level. Not surprisingly, most of the homes shown in this chapter belonged to folks mentioned elsewhere in this book.

What would become known as Woodburn Plantation began in 1790, when Robert Alexander bought 2,000 acres on Old Frankfort Pike just west of Midway from the heirs of Gen. Hugh Mercer. By the mid-1800s, it had become a leading stock farm that greatly improved the quality of Thoroughbred horses, cattle, and other stock. Much of this success was due to the great stallion Lexington (1850–1875), the leading sire for many years. The property remained in the Alexander family for many generations. The original 2,000 acres were sold off in large tracts that became the sites of other successful horse farms in northern Woodford County. The photograph above shows the house that was built around 1848 on the property. Below is the property after the exterior was changed beginning in 1925 by adding columns and painting the residence white.

This is one of the rooms of the Woodburn Plantation house in 1913, when the house and farm that made up Woodburn were owned by A.J.A. Alexander, grandson of the original owner of the estate.

This is believed to be the oldest house remaining in the community of Mortonsville. It was built by H.A. Arnett, probably in the early 1800s, although the exact date is unknown. It is of partial brick and partial stone construction. In 1881, it was sold by Arnett's heirs to Thomas Beasley. It is shown on the 1877 map of Woodford County.

This photograph, taken around 1900, shows the Samuel Black House. Black was a farmer near Troy. The individuals are unidentified, although they are presumably members of the Black family. The house was located near the Troy Presbyterian Church (see page 56), off of today's Route 33 in the southern part of the county. The house is shown on the 1877 map of Woodford County.

Samuel L. Wooldridge (1879–1945) is seen in front of his home, Village View, on High Street in Versailles. At six feet, five inches and over 250 pounds, he was known as "Big Sam." He is shown with some of his foxhounds, of which he was a world-class breeder. Foxhounds from all over North America were shipped to his kennel in Versailles to be bred. The house is still in existence.

This abandoned house was photographed on Scott's Ferry Road. It is included here as an example of what has happened to many of the county's farmhouses. Often referred to as vernacular architecture, these frame houses were built by local craftsmen using local, traditional designs and materials to meet the needs of the local community. While some still exist as modern residences, many have ended up like this one.

Mundy's Landing is located on the Kentucky River at the southern tip of Woodford County and is named for Thomas Mundy, who built a log house overlooking the river before 1800. It was the site of a ferry that crossed the river between Mercer and Woodford Counties. Jeremiah Mundy, Thomas's son, took over his father's business interests and built the impressive two-story white house with double verandas facing the river shown here. The house was operated as a tavern and inn for both river passengers and travelers on the Harrodsburg-Versailles Pike. The village at that time was an important stop for the many steamboats that operated on the river. Because of this river traffic, the village had a general store, warehouses, a coal yard, a sawmill, a post office, and other businesses. The house is currently a private residence and is not visible from the road.

This photograph shows Judge James T. Wilhoit and his wife, Alice Bohon Wilhoit, relaxing at the old Wilhoit homeplace on McCowans Ferry Road sometime around 1900. Judge Wilhoit served as county judge/executive and sheriff of Woodford County. He also served as postmaster of Versailles. Judge Wilhoit died in 1923, and Alice passed in 1929.

The Harris House, at 142 Locust Street near downtown Versailles, is shown around 1880. It was the home of Nathaniel and Margaret Morgan Harris. Nathaniel was a soldier in the Civil War and a cofounder of the Harris-Seller Bank. The house is currently used by a private business.

This c. 1920 photograph of a house on Oregon Road shows the Lancaster family. The 1920 census lists the family as Stonewall Lancaster; his wife, Drusie; and two children, Jack (four years old) and Mary (two). The woman on the left is unidentified. The exact location of the house could not be determined.

Dunvegan is on the Versailles-Midway Road on what was originally part of a 3,000-acre military grant given to Revolutionary War hero Capt. Reuben Twyman. His son Joel Twyman built this Colonial brick home in 1810. It was known as the Twyman Place for decades. In 1900, George MacLeod, who was general manager of the Louisville & Atlantic Railroad, bought the house and 245 acres and renamed it Dunvegan.

This one-and-a-half-story Federal-style house was built in the late 1790s by Revolutionary War hero Jack Jouett (see page 43). After the war, Jouett moved to Kentucky, where he lived in Mercer County for 10 years. In 1797, he moved to Woodford County, settling on 524 acres on Craigs Creek, where he built this house. He lived here until December 1809. One of Jouett's sons was Matthew Jouett, an artist who painted the portraits of several of Kentucky's prominent citizens. The house is owned by Woodford County and is open for public tours. Below is a side view of the house. The stone portion to the rear was originally a detached kitchen. In this pre-renovation photograph, the area has been enclosed by white clapboard. The house has now been restored to its original configuration. (Both, courtesy of Jack Jouett House.)

The Wilson House in Mortonsville was built about 1830 by Benjamin Wilson. The house, still used as a private residence, sits on the hill above where Delaney's Ferry Road crosses Tanner's Creek. Wilson's father, Jeremiah, a Revolutionary War soldier, traded his military land grant in Bourbon County for this property. The house is shown on the 1877 map of Woodford County as belonging to F.S. Wilson, Benjamin's son.

This house had a convenient location near the courthouse. It had lots of overnight guests, but none were there by choice. It was the county jail around 1911. It was built in 1903 to replace the prior 1840s jail. The front of the house, shown here, was the jailer's residence, with the jail cells in the rear of the building. It was torn down in 1995 to make room for the courthouse annex.

Bibliography

Davis, John Steele. *"On the Road Tour" of Southern Woodford County*. Versailles, KY: self-published, 2001.

Estridge, Danna C. *Marking Time in Woodford County, Kentucky*. Versailles, KY: Woodford County Historical Society, 2003.

Kimmerer, Tom. *Woodland Pastures.* kimmerer.com/woodland-bluegrass-nashville/woodland-pastures/ (accessed March 2019).

Kleber, John E., ed. *The Kentucky Encyclopedia*. Lexington, KY: University Press of Kentucky, 1992.

Munson, Dabney G., and Margaret W. Parrish, eds. *Woodford County, Kentucky: The First Two Hundred Years*. Versailles, KY: published by the editors, 1989.

Railey, William E. *History of Woodford County, Kentucky*. Frankfort, KY: Clearfield Company Inc., 1990 (Reprint of 1938 edition).

Sulzer, Elmer G. *Ghost Railroads of Kentucky*. Bloomington, IN: Indiana University Press, 1968.

Woodford Sun. Various articles contained in the files of the Woodford County Historical Society.

Visit us at
arcadiapublishing.com

www.ingramcontent.com/pod-product-compliance
Lightning Source LLC
Chambersburg PA
CBHW062139160426

43191CB00014B/2334